Old NEWRY

by

Alex F. Young, with photographs from the Tommy O'Hanlor

Designed by local architect William Batt, Newry Town Hall was built on a three span bridge over the Clanrye river in 1893 at a cost of £9,000. The reason given for the choice of this unusual and expensive site was that as the river divides Newry between Co. Armagh and Co. Down, the town hall could serve its people from a position of neutrality. There are, however, those who whisper that as buildings which stand over water do not pay rates, the council hoped to make a saving! The classical style building to the right, erected in 1840 for the Newry Savings Bank, was bought by the council in the early 1890s and served as the municipal offices while the town hall was being built. In September 1903 it became the Municipal Technical School. This closed in 1980 and the building then found a new purpose as the town's arts centre and museum.

© Text, Alex F. Young, 2002
First published in the United Kingdom, 2002,
by Stenlake Publishing Limited,
01290 551122
www.stenlake.co.uk

Printed by Blissetts, Roslin Road, Acton, W3 8DH

ISBN 9781840331929

ACKNOWLEDGEMENTS

The author would like to thank the following for their help: Lilian Bradley of Mullaglass Primary School, Austin Smith and Jimmy Davis of the *Newry Reporter*, the Abbey National Building Society, Bertie Flynn, John D.F. Fisher, Desmond Fearon, Robert Grieves, Fr. McCartan, Sister Perpetua McArdle, Viviane Adamson, Paddy Smith, Arthur Mooney, Michael Fairgrieve of Newry Rugby Club, and the staff of Newry Branch Library, Lincoln Central Library and Paisley Central Library.

The publishers wish to thank A.D. Packer for permission to reproduce the photograph on page 47.

FURTHER READING

The books listed below were used by the author during his research. None of them are available from Stenlake Publishing. Those interested in finding out more are advised to contact their local bookshop or reference library.

Ordnance Survey, *Memoirs of Ireland: Parishes of County Down 1, 1834–6*, Institute of Irish Studies, 1990.

E.M. Patterson, *The Great Northern Railway of Ireland*, Oakwood Press, no date.

Tony Canavan, *Frontier Town – Newry*, The Blackstaff Press, Belfast, 1989.

When the Independent Congregation built Ebenezer Chapel in 1825, it was on a developing area of Kildare Street which was later renamed Trevor Hill after the Trevor family. The rough granite building, accommodating 400, cost £500 which was raised by public subscription. Little is known of this congregation which by the early twentieth century had been succeeded in ownership of the building by the Salvation Army. Since this early photograph, the word 'Citadel' has been dropped from its name.

INTRODUCTION

If a town's history is to be found in street names, then Sugar Island, Merchant's Quay, Buttercrane Quay and Corn Market all tell of Newry's history as a trading centre. But this was far in the future when the first settlers took root in one of the oldest settlements in Ireland. Newry's importance was founded on its position both on the main route between Ulster and Leinster and on the Clanrye river on its way to Carlingford Lough and the open sea. With a little imagination we can see how the name derives from the Gaelic *Iubhair Cinn Tragh* – 'yew tree at the head of the strand'.

When St Patrick was sent to Ireland by Pope Celestine in AD 432 and planted his 'Yew Tree at the head of the Strand', he founded not only the embryo settlement that would become Newry, but made converts amongst travellers passing through. In 1144 this connection with St Patrick influenced the Cistercian monks from Co. Louth to build an abbey here, dedicated to St Mary and St Patrick, under the tutelage of Maurice MacLoughlin, King of Ireland, and the abbey gave the town a focus around which to develop. The abbey survived until the mid-sixteenth century when, amongst the many changes wrought by the Reformation, the monks' lands (some 5,500 acres) passed to Nicholas Bagenal, a marshal in King Henry VIII's army. By then the settlement had grown to seventy-two houses, with two salmon weirs and a mill. A period of relative peace and prosperity followed. In 1689, however, while in the hands of the Duke of Berwick and a Jacobite army of 2,000 men, it was set ablaze to deny the advancing Williamite army, under the Duke of Schlomberg, shelter and food. The six surviving houses became the nucleus of the town in today's layout.

When coal workings opened in Co. Tyrone at the beginning of the eighteenth century, the idea of a canal between Newry and Lough Neagh was mooted and a survey commissioned in 1703. The surveyor, Captain Francis Neill, reported favourably and estimated the cost at £20,000. Several thwarted starts were made before work began in 1730 under the supervision of Richard Cassels – the first of a number of overseers of the scheme before its completion in 1742. With eighteen miles of waterway and fifteen locks to raise it 80 feet above sea level at Poyntzpass, it was for its time a major feat of engineering. In 1765 the waterway to Carlingford Lough was completed.

Successful as the canal was, a rival was on the horizon in the form of the expanding rail system. In 1845 the Newry & Enniskillen Railway Company was formed to link the two towns through Armagh and Clones, a distance of seventy-two miles, but took seven years to complete the three and a half mile line to Goraghwood. Although the railways won out and the canal system fell into a gradual decline, Newry, now an established trading centre, weathered the transition and continued to prosper.

In the twentieth century both the canal and railway would give way to road transport. After years of decline, the canal fell further and further into decrepitude and was closed in 1949. Beeching would see to the slaughter of the railways in the 1960s.

With the exception of the canal, the dock (which was handling over 100,000 tons of goods per annum by the mid-nineteenth century) and the railway, Newry had few large employers until 1845 when John Grubb Richardson chose Bessbrook, two miles from the town, for his linen spinning mill. A Quaker, Richardson was one of the early proponents of the model village built around the factory (Robert Owen had already established one at New Lanark in Scotland's Clyde Valley). Richardson's philosophy was to 'control our people and to do them good in every sense'. An alternative view would say that this meant he got more work from them by keeping them from the 'demon drink'. The village around the mill was not large enough to house all his workers and such were the number travelling each day from Newry that the Bessbrook and Newry Tramway was built and opened in 1885. It remained in service until 1948.

Having survived both a post-war decline in trade and industry and the 'Troubles', Newry's star is again in the ascendancy. In March 2002, as part of the celebrations to mark the fiftieth anniversary of the accession of Queen Elizabeth, Newry – as well as Lisburn in Co. Antrim – was granted city status. Of the forty-two applications made for this status, five – Newry, Lisburn, Carrickfergus, Coleraine and Craigavon – were from Northern Ireland. Among the assets mentioned in Newry's citation were its architectural inheritance and that currently it has the highest number of new businesses in Northern Ireland.

Taken from the Armaghdown Bridge in front of the town hall, this photograph shows Sugar Island on the left while in the centre background is the courthouse with its fine cupola. Trevor Hill is on the right. Adams' paint and wallpaper shop, Trimble the tailor (and post office), and the barber's shop on the corner of Basin Walk have given way to Friar Tuck's restaurant and off-licence. 'The Russian Trophy', a cannon captured from the Russians during the Crimean War (1854–56) and gifted to the town shortly afterwards, stood by the riverside until 1938 when it was moved onto the bridge to make way for the war memorial. Bearing no individual names, the cenotaph features only the simple inscription, 'Memorial to the World Wars'.

Sugar Island, where cargoes of sugar were unloaded in times past, viewed from the Sugar Island Bridge to the Canal Street junction and the Newry Tea House. Many shops and business have come and gone here since this picture was taken in the 1920s, and, of course, the volume of one-way traffic which now flows towards the bridge has greatly increased.

Much has changed since this photograph of Canal Street was taken from Sugar Island in 1930. O'Hare's wine and spirit store is now the Hermitage public house and the waitresses of the Newry Tea House have been replaced by the mechanics of the Volkswagen dealer, P. & R. Motor Sales, whose cars have in turn replaced the horses and carts.

The buildings of Merchants Quay, seen here from Monaghan Street Bridge, served the canal and its commercial traffic. When this photograph was taken in the 1930s it was still the commercial heart of Newry. While there is no information available about the Newry Coal & Salt Co., the Custom and Revenue Office (in the centre of the picture) is now gone. O'Hagan's coal and hardware store at No. 18 Merchants Quay survived until the 1940s. This part of the Newry Canal closed in 1956, a victim of the general decline of the canal system across the country, and most of these buildings have either been demolished or redeveloped.

Built on the junction of Canal Quay and New Street in 1873 by local builder John O'Hare, Robert Sands' Clanrye Mill replaced an earlier mill which had been destroyed by fire the previous year. It was Newry's largest grain mill. Described as 'an essay in brickwork', architect William Watson took the Lombardo–Venetian style of the 1866 Riverside Reformed Presbyterian Church (on the right) as his reference. The mill is now boarded up and the reflective water of the canal basin has been built over and replaced by a car park.

When the Newry Canal opened in 1742 industrial and commercial ventures flourished, although with one notable exception – the Ulster White Linen Hall. Built in 1783 on the canal's west bank at a cost of £14,000, it was designed solely as a market place for locally produced linen but for some reason failed to be a success and struggled to the end of the century when it was bought by the government and converted to a barracks. The eight acre site then had two blocks for officers, six for other ranks, a hospital and ancillary buildings. The army later relinquished it and in March 1928 it was purchased by Newry Urban Council for £1,200. They converted it to housing for fifty 'poorer class' families who paid a rent of 3/6d per week. Announcing the purchase, the council expressed their relief at beating a Belfast syndicate which planned to build a greyhound racing track. Councillor W.R. Bell hoped they would never see greyhound racing in Newry as he 'did not think it was for the public good'. Linen Hall Square survived until the late 1960s when it was cleared to make way for the new housing of Mourne View Park. Barrack Street and the East Gateway Arch remain as reminders of bygone days.

Kildare Street looking towards Trevor Street, with the courthouse and the Corry Monument beyond Murphy's bridge on the left (this was also known as the 'Stone Bridge'). The riverside wall by which the messenger boy stands was rebuilt and raised as a flood defence during 2001. The buildings from the right have changed little since this photograph was taken.

As Kildare Street swept to the left, the shops and businesses turned to the banks of Trevor Hill. The first shop on the right, the Ulster Clothing Co. on the corner of Hill Street, was followed by Newry Meat Market in a row which ran up to Trevor Hill. On Trevor Hill the first building, a three storey house, was built in 1770 by Andrew Thompson. Next to it is the granite front of the Northern Banking Company's premises and then there is a four storey, mid-nineteenth century house. Behind the tree on the far left is an 1860s bonded warehouse which later became St Colman's Hall.

Trevor Hill, looking to the Corry Monument where Downshire Road forks to the left and Sandy's Street to the right. In the left foreground, the granite and stucco finished courthouse stands behind its ornamental railings. It was built in 1843 to replace the original courthouse in Margaret Square which was lost when the square was opened to Monaghan Street. Designed by the Newry architect Thomas Duff, it is admired for its 'compact elegance' and was renovated in 1994.

A view of Sandy's Street from the grounds of the courthouse, with a convoy of wagons wending its way from the canal. The three storey house to the right, on the Trevor Hill junction, was later the Copper Grill, who advertised their 'Fine Food . . . Efficient Service', and is now the Brass Monkey public house. From there the mid-nineteenth century listed terrace running to Talbot Street and Windsor Hill is broken by the opening into Heather Park where the United Irishmen were executed in 1798. On the left stands the Corry Monument, erected in 1877 to the memory of Trevor Corry, a magistrate in Newry for thirty-five years. His family home, Derrymore, stands two miles east of Newry and is now cared for by the National Trust. The monument, like the railway bridge on Camlough Road, illustrates the Victorian predilection for 'Egyptian' style stonework. Beyond the monument are the First Newry Presbyterian Church, built in 1829, and the Methodist Church of 1841.

Sandy's Street, festooned with bunting for the coronation of Queen Elizabeth on Tuesday, 2 June 1953. The *Newry Reporter* that day carried the headline 'Prayers for the Queen then Fun and Games' and the celebrations began with a 9.30 a.m. service in the town hall for all of Newry's congregations, led by the Rev William McAdam of the First Presbyterian Church. The afternoon brought fancy dress competitions in the Grammar School sports field where, in the children's classes, Barbara and Sandra Auterson (billed as 'Two Little Girls in Blue') were judged the prettiest. In the adults' section the results for the most original costume were: 1st, Mrs McCormack ('Television Set'); 2nd, Mrs Grills ('Ministry of Food Demonstrator'); 3rd, Mrs C. Grills ('Coronation Weather'). Marches and parades led by the Commons Silver and Reed Band, the Hunter Moore Memorial Band and the Frontier Pipe Band, ran all day and there was a final parade to Ashgrove for a bonfire and firework display. The day ended where it had started, in the town hall, with revellers celebrating through to the early hours of Wednesday morning.

From the head of Sandy's Street the coronation decorations ran up into Talbot Street. Taken in the week leading up to Coronation Day, this photograph shows Vera Cox, then in her mid-forties, outside her house at No. 11. The third youngest in a family of fourteen, Vera (neé Patterson) married Sammy Cox, a bus conductor, in the early 1930s and lived in this house until her death in January 1985. The parked car belonged to her neighbour, Albert Martin.

The Orange Hall, Newry.

Built as a town house by the Marquis of Downshire in the early nineteenth century, Downshire House stood on the elevated west side of the Belfast road (now Downshire Road). After passing through a number of owners it was bought by the Orange Institution in 1920 when increasing membership, and a newly founded women's section, forced them from their hall at the courthouse. They renamed it the 'Henry Thomson Memorial Orange Hall' to commemorate the late Henry Thomson, DL, JP, a prominent Orangeman and Unionist MP for Newry between 1880 and 1886, who was born in the house. In the early 1980s the property was sold for development and demolished. The site was used for a garage premises and a new Orange hall was also then built there.

16

A view of Hill Street from the Kildare Street junction, with Kinnear the grocer – also famed for their meats – and the Newry Nursery – equally famed for their garden seeds – on the left. On the right were the premises of John Mercer the jeweller, who bought the business in 1900 from Edward Sloan who had traded there since 1886.

Kennedy & Ford occupied this shop at No. 69 Hill Street for a short time in the early twentieth century, being there by 1902 but gone by the start of the First World War when it became (and remains) the Shelbourne Restaurant. Earlier occupants included Edward Caulfield & Son's bakery (1847–54) and the printer Collins & Collins. Internally there were two shops – ladies' millinery, dresses and mantles to the left, and tailoring and outfits for gentlemen on the right. The tailor on the right would no doubt have insisted on being photographed with his tape measure.

Hill Street viewed from Margaret Square and looking to Sugar Island, before the days of the motor car and the Green Clock (the timepiece which stood in the centre of the square, directly in the foreground of the picture). The Victoria Hotel on the left corner later became the Ulster Bank, and on the right O'Hagan & O'Hare's Medical Hall (O'Hare was added at the turn of the century) became J. & J. Griffith, who were in the business of providing 'something very attractive in men's wear' by the 1930s. It is now a branch of the Edinburgh Woollen Mill.

Margaret Square, with Hill Street to the left and Margaret Street to the right, was established as a new development in the 1760s. J. Warnock & Co. of No. 2 Margaret Square were printers and booksellers from as early as 1812 when Alex Wilkinson first printed the *Newry Telegraph* from those premises. The Abbey National Building Society bought them in 1981. The sign of the Golden Teapot café can just be seen on the right.

The 1834–36 Ordnance Survey *Memoirs of Ireland* gives Hill Street's length as 580 yards. That length may not have altered greatly since, but the street's appearance certainly did in 1978 when it became Northern Ireland's first pedestrian priority street. The terrace on the left includes the Cathedral Presbytery, the Provincial Bank of Ireland (now First Trust Bank) built in 1905, and the Crown Post Office. The Cathedral of Saint Patrick and Saint Colman on the right was built in 1829.

Hill Street in the 1940s – when the traffic ran both ways – looking north towards Marcus Street. The three storey post office building was built at a cost of £5,700 and finished in Newry granite to complement the cathedral. It opened in March 1900. Alas, it fell foul of a modernisation programme in the early 1960s when the rough granite frontage was replaced with steel, plastic and polished granite slabs. Next door, Andrew McClure's pharmacy, resembling a branch of Kodak the photographic company, typifies chemists' shops of the period. On the corner to Marcus Street, on the left, was the painter and decorator's shop of Joseph Ward which was run by his daughter Minnie until the 1960s. On the right, Henry McAteer's cabinet maker's shop opened in 1886. It was run by his son, Michael Joseph, until the 1950s.

This building was erected as A.R. Walker's new mill about 1880 and took the site of Robert McClelland's blacksmith's forge. Bounded by Mill Street and Lower Water Street, this view shows the Hill Street frontage with the cathedral on the left. The photograph shows the damage caused by a fire on 8 December 1910 when it was occupied by Robert Sands' grain store and the print works of the *Newry Reporter*. The alarm was raised just after 3.00 a.m. when the print room was found full of smoke. The fire brigade turned out, but a fire of this scale, fanned by a strong wind, was beyond their resources. The press reported, rather ungenerously, that 'their efforts were absolutely useless'. Added to this, low water pressure rendered their hoses ineffectual above the ground floor. By 6.00 a.m. the conflagration was at its highest and the scarlet glow could be seen from Kilkeel, Rathfriland and Newtonhamilton. In a foolhardy attempt to assess the fire, Brigade Captain R.F. Maginnis took Fireman James Fegan into the building at an early stage, but was called away, leaving Fegan to his fate under falling beams and machinery. The only casualty, he left a widow and five children. Most of the shell of the building was later demolished, although part of it was incorporated into a garden attached to the cathedral.

Mill Street viewed from Ballybot Bridge in late 1935. The Mall goes off to the left, with Orr the chemist opposite Murray the printer, while Con McNulty's public house, McIlroy the butcher and Daly's wallpaper and paint shop are at St Mary's Street junction on the right.

The Christian Brothers School, at the 'Car Stands' on the junction of Margaret Street and the Mall, was built as a two storey building in the 1860s. One of three schools they ran concurrently in the town, it had two classrooms holding fifty to sixty pupils on each floor. Within a decade the third level was added for a science department, an art room and a dormitory for boarders. The building's stone carved insignia bore a Celtic cross and the motto, *Facere et Docere* ('to do and to teach'). In 1938 the pupils were moved to Courtney Hill and the building lay vacant until the Second World War when it became a food rationing centre. It was demolished in the late 1940s.

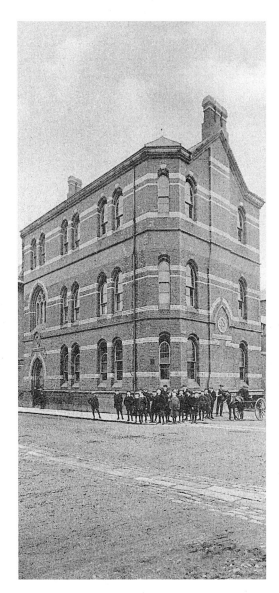

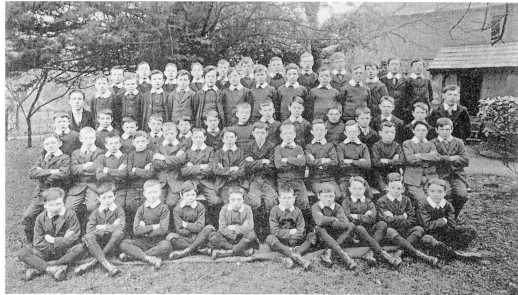

A group of pupils of the Christian Brothers' School pose for the camera in the garden behind the Master's House on Abbey Way. The site of the house has a long history. Traditionally, it is here that St Patrick planted the yew tree, and is also where the Cistercian monks had an abbey until the Reformation. In the early nineteenth century Isaac Corry lived in the house. The Christian Brothers came to Newry in 1851 and took this property for one of their schools following a short spell in Canal Street. It served until the pupils were moved to the school on Courtney Hill. After that the building lay derelict for a time, but was saved by the enterprising Clanrye Abbey Developments, a group of Brothers and locals whose renovation efforts won them an award from the Royal Institution of British Architects in 1987. In the days before state sponsored education, when this photograph was taken, the school was fee paying, except in cases of hardship when families only had to pay what they could afford.

Elsewhere in Britain the business of funeral undertaking is traditionally linked to carpenters, but in Ireland, as we see here with William O'Neill's premises in Sugar Island, it could also be carried out by wine and spirit dealers! Could the poster in his window have been for a 'danse macabre'?

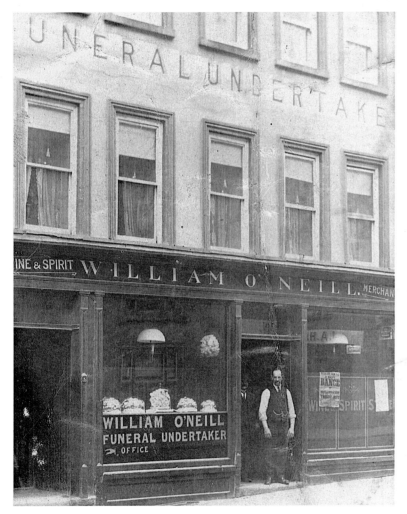

Thomas P. Ledlie & Co., ladies and gents outfitters of North Street, served Newry's better dressed Edwardians – the gentleman in bowler, tails and buttonhole could have been the manager or a customer. Unusually for a retail trader, the staff 'lived in', occupying rooms at the rear. Brought down in the 1950s, this area of North Street was rebuilt as housing. The photograph comes from a postcard sent on 31 August 1910 by Lou Cunningham to his parents in Cork. Lou had just arrived in Newry and was not happy – 'Dear Mother and Father, arrived safely. Train twenty-five minutes late. I wish I was at home again.'

Parked at its terminus outside the Technical College in College Square East, Belfast, in the late 1920s, this thirty seater Associated Daimler omnibus was one of a hundred bought by the newly formed Belfast Omnibus Company. R.J. Poots of Dromore had started the Belfast to Newry service in 1924, and was one of forty operators taken over by the newly formed B.O.C. in 1927. The Newry terminus was in Marcus Square.

A view of Dublin Bridge and Bridge Street running up to the Dublin Road. Owen Hollywood's pub is on the right and the office of Joseph Fisher and Sons, shipping merchant, is on the left. The swing bridge was built as a joint venture by the town and the Newry Navigation Co. in the 1830s, but following the closure of the canal through the town in March 1956, it was replaced by the present fixed bridge in 1958.

At Dublin Bridge the canal opened out into Albert Basin and here ships met the local barges. Joseph Fisher's office is on the right in this view.

S.S. *Pine* and another Fisher Fleet vessel discharging coal at Albert Basin in the 1920s. Built by John Fullerton & Co. of Paisley, Scotland, at a cost of £7,300, the *Pine* was launched on 25 September 1907 and her fitting completed in November for delivery to the Frontier Town Steamship Co. (owned by Fisher) at Newry. On 12 November 1936, while at anchor in Carlingford Lough, she was struck by the steamer *Olive* and sank, the *Olive* rescuing her crew. Refloated, she was bought by Samuel Gray in partnership with Isaac Stewart, both of Belfast, and served another twenty years. On 14 June 1955 she arrived in the Firth of Clyde off Troon, where she ended her days in the hands of the West of Scotland Shipbreaking Co.

Purchased in 1919 by the Dundalk & Newry Steam Packet Company for the Newry to Liverpool general cargo service, the S.S. *Kittiwake* is seen here berthed at Albert Basin. She was scrapped in 1927.

Owned by the Dundalk & Newry Steam Packet Co., the S.S. *Iveagh*, pictured here in Albert Basin, plied a regular passenger and cargo service between Newry and Liverpool. Built on the Clyde in 1892, she was in service when the 'Dundalk and Newry' was acquired by the British and Irish Steam Packet Co. in 1927.

The M.V. *Karri* arriving at Albert Basin with a cargo of coal, captained either by John O'Keefe or William Cahoon. Launched in June 1938 from Scott's Yard at Bowling on the Clyde, she was powered by an eight cylinder oil engine from Humboldt–Deutz of Cologne. She was to be an unlucky ship. On 15 January 1942, while bringing coal from Liverpool to Dublin, she struck a mine and was seriously damaged by fire. In 1957 she was sold to a Greek shipping company and ended her days in 1976, sinking off Marseille in heavy weather after her engine failed.

Two Fisher Fleet steam coasters leaving the Newry Canal at Victoria Locks in the early 1930s. The first one has just passed through and the lock is being prepared for the second while a topsail schooner also waits to depart.

Monaghan Street looking towards Catherine Street in the spring of 1920. Just squeezing into the left is the Armaghdown Bar and next to it is the shop best remembered as McArdle's bicycle shop, but now owned by Ross Carr, estate agents. The first of the overlooking chimneys served the Central Laundry and the second, the Mill.

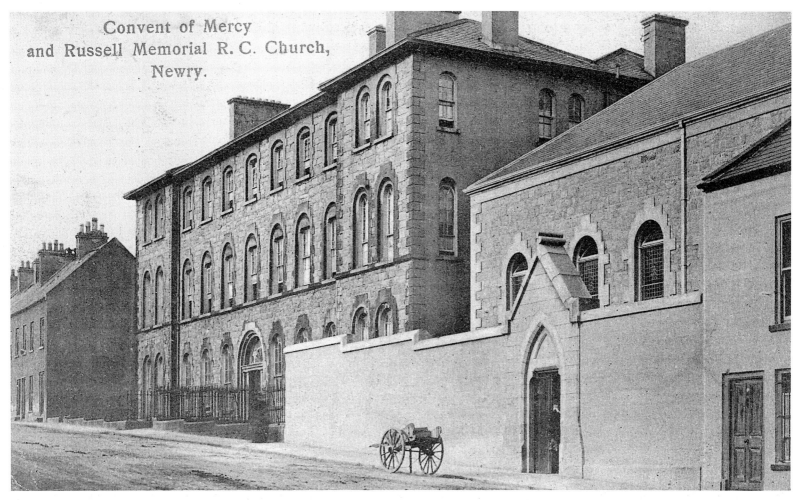

Convent of Mercy
and Russell Memorial R. C. Church,
Newry.

The Sisters of Mercy, founded in Dublin by Catherine McAuley in 1831, came to Newry in 1855. Like the Christian Brothers, they occupied a house in Canal Street, but this proved to be too small. The foundation stone for this building in Catherine Street was laid on 27 August 1860. With a frontage of 100 feet and a depth of 50 feet, the four storey building was designed by Burke of Dublin and built by the Newry builder Byrne at a cost of £4,000 which was raised by town collections and sermons. On the right of the photograph is the Russell Memorial, or Emmanuel Chapel, consecrated in July 1904, and named after Lady Russell of Killowen who gifted £2,000. Her sister-in-law, Mother Emmanuel Russell, made a supplement of £1,000.

Standing as it does in rich farm land, it is surprising that Newry did not have its own agricultural show until 1901. However, by 1908 the Newry Agricultural Society held one Ireland's best shows, attracting the finest of exhibits among which, that year, were 215 horses and four donkeys, 175 cattle and seventy-nine sheep, and an entourage of goats, swine, poultry and eggs. The spring of 1908 had melted into a fine warm summer – until the morning of the show, which brought a blight of cold drizzling rain. The show, which was opened by the Right Honourable, the Earl of Kilmorey, KB, of Mourne Park, almost brought ruin to the Society due to low gate receipts. In 2001 it was cancelled altogether due to the outbreak of foot and mouth disease in Britain.

Dating from the late nineteenth century, this postcard, which bears the caption 'R. Hornsby & Sons Ltd, Grantham – Garden Plough – Newry, Ireland', was used by this Lincolnshire company's depot at 24 Lower Ormond Quay, Dublin, to advertise their products in Ireland. Founded in 1828 by Richard Hornsby (1790–1868), the company's reputation grew on their quality workmanship and innovative engineering (they had a heavy oil engine in commercial production five years before Dr Rudolf Diesel's appeared in 1896). The garden plough shown here was one of ninety-four different plough types produced and sold in countries ranging from Romania to South Africa. 'A first rate plough for smallholdings and light bogland. A pony or a couple of donkeys can manage it easily. The price is £2.15/-, or with Riding Breast, i.e. a seat, for potatoes or roots, £3.2/6. May we send you one?'

Formed as a flute and drum band in the 1870s, St Joseph's Band won the All Ireland Championship four times in the 1880s and '90s. From holding their practice sessions in an old house in James Street, they joined forces with the Independent Club to become the Independent National and St Joseph's Brass & Reed Band, and moved to the club's premises in Kilmorey Street. In the United Kingdom Championships of 1897 they were joint first and came third the following year. The 1920s brought more achievements, winning the Championship of Great Britain and Ireland at Manchester in October 1923, as well as the Dublin event in 1924 and 1928, when this photograph was taken. They remained a strength until the early 1950s when membership fell away. *Front row* (left to right): G. Fegan, P. Kennedy, D. McGivern, J. Burke; *second row*: J. Foley, J. Ruddy, W. McCormack, T. Ruddy (conductor), Rev. Dan Toman, C. Crothers, H. Holt, P. Burke; *third row*: T. Ruddy, G. Campbell, J. Lyons, P. Mallon, J. Hempinstall, T. Quinn, J. Brown, V. Matthews, P. McAlinden, D. Foley, J. Donnelly; *fourth row*: J. McGivern, J. Campbell, J. McCartney, O. Donnelly, P. Gilliam, T. Mulligan, J. O'Hanlon, P. Campbell, T. Hanley, W. Brown, J. McGawley; *back row*: J. Campbell, C. Devine, P. Loy, S. Wright, B. Mooney, F. McCourt.

In 1903 Newry Rowing Club, founded in 1873, became the first provincial rowing club to row at the sport's premier event, Henley, and were the first in Ireland to form a ladies team. This photograph was taken in 1926 outside the clubhouse on the middle bank between the river and the canal. The two coxed four teams are flanked by Mr H.J. McConville (left), president, and Mr Joseph Fisher (future solicitor and senator), secretary. The ladies are, *back row*: Eileen Thompson, Una Hennessey, unknown, unknown; *middle row*: unknown, Peggy Muntz, unknown, Dorothy Sinclair; *front row*: unknown, Netta Fisher. Despite the waters of the river and the canal being suitable for training to Olympic level, the club faded out in the 1930s, with the derelict clubhouse being demolished soon after. Only since the 1990s has interest been rekindled.

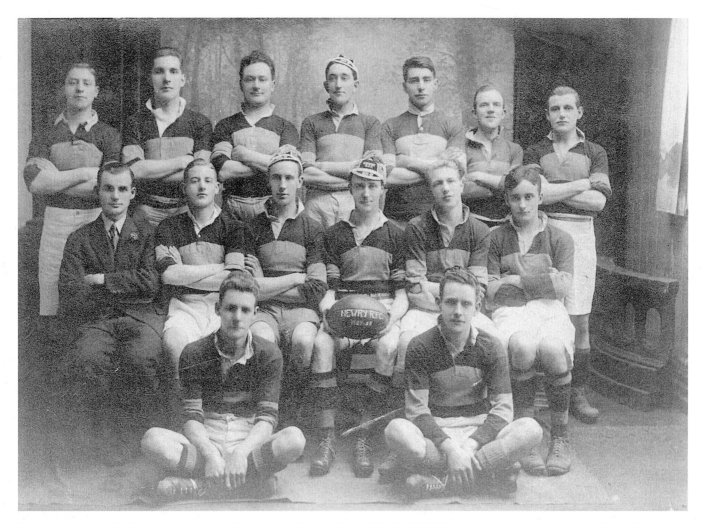

Initially with no ground, no clubhouse, and at times few players, Newry Rugby Football Club has struggled to survive since its beginnings in 1925. This photograph of the 1927/28 team shows fourteen of the players ready to take the field. Wound up in the late 1930s, it was 1961 before the club reformed and the soccer club gave them use of a pitch at the Showgrounds. After playing at a number pitches they settled at Crobane in 1972, where they now have a clubhouse.

Newry Town Football Club's team for the season 1936/37. *Back row* (left to right): W.J. (Billy) Redfern, A. Collins, H. McCaw, J. Gunther, R. Johnston, J. Twomey, N. McIvor, G. Black, H. Holborn, P. Duffy; *front row*: D. Thomson, D. McCart, J.W. Syddal, W. Whitehouse, E. Rigby. Founded in 1923, the club itself has not, as yet, attained as many honours as some who have played for it. Of those included in this photograph, Billy Redfern was regarded as the best centre forward of his time and was the top scorer in the Irish League that season with forty-eight goals (he was not dressed in a strip for the photo due to injury) and Jimmy Twomey played for the national team. A generation later the team fielded goalkeeper Pat Jennings who earned 119 caps and after whom Jennings Park is named.

In June 1904 local steeplejack Jemmy Gill became a fugitive, the toast of Newry, and a celebrity throughout Britain. Sought by the police for a minor misdemeanour, Jemmy escaped and made for Sugar Island where he barricaded himself in the boiler house of the disused factory chimney he should have been demolishing. Within days, crowds were gathering and the *Newry Reporter* (which also published a supplement on him) was telegraphing Jemmy's exploits across Britain. These included hoisting a flag and setting off a firework display. Two weeks passed and it was only after he was injured in a fall that he was arrested and taken home. He then escaped again and returned to his eyrie where he stayed for another week before being rearrested.

The west bank of the Newry Canal, south of Albert Basin, looking towards the Dublin Road and what is now Drumalane Park and Fathom Park (Fathom derives from *Fiodha-Dun*, the 'forest castle' built a mile and a half south in 1563). Beside the tow path, and the boys with their donkey, ran the track of the Dundalk, Newry & Greenore Railway Co. which opened in 1873.

Clohogue Church, Newry.

On its hilltop a mile and a half south of Newry and commanding a fine view over the town, Cloughoge Church of the Sacred Heart serves the parish of Upper Killeavy. Built by P.J. Neary and Felix O'Hare of Newry to a design by the architects Ashlin and Coleman of Dawson Street, Dublin, its building drew on talents and materials from far and wide. Topped with a roof of Westmoreland slate, the altar marble came from Carrara and Siena in Italy, the mosaics were by artists from Rome, and the stain glass windows by Mayer of Munich. The foundation stone was laid in 1911 and although it was dedicated on Easter Sunday 1916, it was not consecrated until September 1930 when the final bill was paid. This photograph of 1915 shows the work in progress, with the house, which now stands to the left, at foundation stage.

Mullaglass School on Goragh Road, three miles north of Newry, has a long history. The 1821 census shows that at that time forty-two year old Owen Mallon was teaching sixteen boys and eight girls (today the roll consists of forty-two boys and thirty-eight girls). This photograph shows the then new schoolhouse and teacher's residence, completed in 1908 and funded by public subscription through the Mullaglass School Building Fund. The parish had just taken over the responsibility from Captain Roger Hall of Narrow-Water.

The custom post, looking north, on the main Belfast – Newry – Dublin road at Kileen in 1936. A busy crossing, it was served by Maxwell's shop which offered teas, confectionery and tobacco, as well as petrol and oil. The group consists of customs officers, a bus driver and conductor, and two RUC officers. The boy in front of the lorry could have been selling cigarettes or lucky white heather. Found to be in the wrong position, the boundary post was later moved eight yards north.

A Bessbrook and Newry Tramway Company's tram at Edward Street Station, Newry, in the early twentieth century. The three mile narrow gauge (3 feet) electrified line to Bessbrook was opened at a cost of £15,000 in October 1885. This was two years after a similar tramway had opened between Portrush and the Giant's Causeway and while this served tourism to the Causeway, the Co. Armagh service mostly carried workers from Newry to the mills at Bessbrook and home again. Coincidentally both lines were officially closed in 1949, although the last tram on the Newry and Bessbrook actually left Newry on 10 January 1948.

Egyptian Arch, Newry.

M. 254.

Built for the Dublin & Belfast Junction Railway Company in 1851 by William Dargan of Belfast, to a design by Sir John MacNeill, the 'Egyptian Arch' carried the railway over Camlough Road. A major contractor, William Dargan built not only many miles of railway throughout Ireland, but also the bridges and viaducts over which they passed. McNeill had been Professor of Engineering at Trinity College, Dublin, until he joined the railway builders. In its day it was a striking and, for a time, fashionable design.